OCCASIONALLY PETTY

WINNIPEG

OCCASIONALLY PETTY

Michelle Lietz

Occasionally Petty

Design by Matthew Stevens and M. C. Joudrey.
Layout by Matthew Stevens and M. C. Joudrey.
Photography Alethea Phillips .

Published by At Bay Press April 2022.

Library and Archives Canada cataloguing in publication is available upon request.

ISBN 978-1-988168-59-3

Printed and bound in Canada.

This book is printed on acid free paper that is 100% recycled ancient forest friendly (100% post-consumer recycled).

We acknowledge the generous support of the Canada Council for the Arts and the Manitoba Arts Council.

Canada Council for the Arts | Conseil des arts du Canada

MANITOBA ARTS COUNCIL | CONSEIL DES ARTS DU MANITOBA

First Edition

1 0 9 8 7 6 5 4 3 2 1

atbaypress.com

ACKNOWLEDGMENTS

I should begin, of course, with my own position and my gratitude for the lands on which I have found myself over the course of my life. I was born in the occupied homelands of the Pottawatomi, Wyandotte, Odawa, and Anishinaabeg, and I lived there for most of my life, with a brief stint in Treaty 1 territory of Winnipeg, homeland to the Dakota, Dene, Métis, Anishinaabeg, Oji-Cree and Cree Nations. I didn't live in Winnipeg for very long, but I was there when this collection first began.

My father came from a family that was half European settler and half Middle Eastern immigrant. This was rarely discussed in my childhood. My father used to just tell me he was "American," as if that answered all questions. My mother was the opposite of my father in this and many other important ways, ensuring that even from a young age I knew I was Yaqui, despite how far we were from the deserts of what is now Mexico, Arizona, and California. I didn't know any other Indigenous kids (or adults for that matter), but my mom took me to powwow regularly from a young age, and I at least got to experience some aspects of Anishinaabe culture very early on. She gave me more of our history and culture than her father gave to her, and I'm endlessly grateful for it. My family has never had enrollment status, but this never changed how I saw the world, or how the world saw me. I refer to myself often as diasporic Indigenous, and I'm constantly grateful for the many kinships I have formed over the years with Indigenous folks all over Turtle Island who have welcomed me into their homelands for however long I could stay.

I am grateful to my family, both blood relations and found family, without whom I could not have survived this world as long as I have. I could never say in a dedication all that my mother has done for me, but I think it's enough to say that she is undoubtedly my best friend. My sisters mean everything to me, both the ones I was born to and the ones I found along the way. Lauren, my first chosen sister, helped me imagine a future and grow into the kind of person I wanted to be, while loving me even at my weirdest. Amber helped me fight for a hopeful future and gave me a place to fit in I didn't think I'd ever have. My grad-school gang in particular—Jamel, Adam, and David back home, Grace, Jordan, and Jack in Winnipeg—kept me honest, and helped rekindle my passion when I felt it flicker.

I'm extra grateful to Adam and David, who read the early versions of this collection and workshopped with me for hours in bars, basements, and that one time on the sand dunes. I couldn't have gotten so far without you.

I'm grateful for my teachers, especially Lori and Tony; thank you for encouraging my voice and vision.

OPENING CHORDS

Music has informed and sustained my life in ways nothing else compares to, and it holds a special kind of magic that embodies memory in ways that move beyond temporality. The people who know me well can tell what mood I'm in by the playlist I'm listening to.

In April of 1989, Tom Petty released his first solo album (even though most of The Heartbreakers collaborated on it) titled *Full Moon Fever*. This was also the month I was born, when "Free Fallin'" was brand new. And these were the sounds I heard when sitting in a living room picture window trying to get rid of jaundice. I grew to love the music that filled my early years and was heavily influenced by my parents even in what I listen to now. Although Tom Petty was a favorite of my father's, he was content with the greatest hits, and over the years I became more familiar with Tom's words than my father. As far as I'm concerned, Tom has a song for everything, and I turn to him at my best and worst times. Because of this, many of my formative memories are rooted within the chords.

After the 2016 US election, my father stopped speaking to me. I tried many times to repair what was broken, but as the year wore on, the break grew wider. Eventually he cut me out entirely. Not long after, on October 2, 2017, Tom Petty died, and this project was born out of the compounding grief I felt from two very different losses.

The collection starts with my 10th birthday and ends shortly after my 30th, but it isn't linear in between. And while there are many themes flowing in and out and across these works, the only true consistency is they all start with Tom's words. When I started this project, I was just trying to feel better; I compiled a list of his songs that matter the most to me in my own custom curated playlist, and as I listened and grieved, these poems poured out. It began as a means of confronting my grief, but also became a way of mapping my own journey from survival to survivance. When I sat down to construct this work, I wanted to do so in a way that combines musical, poetic, and Indigenous storytelling traditions. I could not have predicted where this would go, but the ride was unforgettable.

Should a reader wish for easy access to the songs which set the mood for any given poem, that playlist can be found on Spotify by scanning the QR code to your left.

PROGRAM

The First Song

"I'm gonna free fall out into nothin'

gonna leave this world for a while"

The joke is old—

worn down through decades of use,

you still tell it

like I don't know the punchline.

Once,

on a birthday that aligned

with some famous rebirth,

along a California road

I pointed towards

Ventura Boulevard—

"you know,

like the song"

and you laughed,

made the same joke

about births

and songs I knew

before words—

and I wondered at the irony

that you could make

the same old joke,

marvel at my memory,

forgetting the day.

An elbow in my side,

a conspiratory grin

in the backseat, she said,

"Hey, know what today is?"

As if I could forget.

Driving Lessons

"runnin' down a dream

that never would come to me

workin' on a mystery

goin' wherever it leads"

Car dancing

is a skill

slowly acquired over

years of steering wheel tapping,

air guitars at stop lights,

and an open road

offering endless possibility,

always familiar

in the limitless way

new roads

remind me

of coming home.

I never could write funny,

but I want to talk about laughter—

I know

half my road trip humor

comes from you.

I still laugh,

when I can remember you

drumming on the steering wheel,

radiant sunshine

always encouraging both of us

to *turn the radio loud,*

sing obnoxiously,

unapologetically

to prove it doesn't matter

how bad we were at it.

And I'd close my eyes

at the sound of a harmonica—
always my weakness.
I laugh now,
remembering
drumming on the steering wheel,
windows down,
air guitar in the car
and tailgating—
while telling me to
always keep my hands
at ten and two.

See, my father,
he was always more
‘do as I say,
not as I do’
spoke in lessons but
never told me stories
and I learned more

from watching him

than I ever did

from listening.

My mother once told me

we both think of our fathers

when that song plays,

hers on a California highway,

another Del in the passenger's seat,

and I wonder

if they were both running.

The funny thing is

I still tell people

my dad used to say he invented the air guitar.

Deer Crossing

"Real love is a man's salvation

the weak ones fall

the strong carry on"

You know,

when I was a kid,

I fell in love

so easily.

I often lived

vicariously

through someone else's stories,

lost in worlds

I rarely saw myself in.

There's a story my people used to tell

about a deer
who had the power
to turn invisible—
such power
kept it alive
long past its prime.
People always assume
there's some easy lesson
in such a story—
at the end, usually—
and the end
of the invisible deer
seems anticlimactic;
old and ready to die,
the deer reveals itself
to the hunters who,
over these many years,
never gave up the chase.
The hunters, unimpressed with

the meat left on the bones

turn, and leave.

So maybe there's a lesson

about chasing—

the fantasy preferable to reality—

a professor of mine once said,

when I told him the story,

that he could see

a metaphor of women,

their beauty and power

lessening over the years

but when I close my eyes

picture that deer,

I see intelligent

gentle eyes,

think of all the times

deer have showed us the way,

through mountains, valleys and

fields of wildflowers.

I’m reminded, sometimes—

survival means

becoming your own ghost,

visible only

to those who already know

how to see.

Road Trip

"I was born with something down inside of me
and it's carried me over, delivered me
yeah delivered me, I'm standing at your gate
just out of reach of the hands of fate"

As long as I've known her
my grandmother has been
a hard woman—rough
around the edges
love you didn't often hear
but could always taste
in homemade bread,
fresh coffee
warm artichoke dip.

My grandmother owned a bar
in a small town—
as familiar as the Buick
I grew up riding in,
first as a child,
my memory fuzzy,
limited mostly to that time
my mother gutted a deer
in the snow,
strapped it to the back
of that black Buick,
and I watched it
the entire way home.
We took that same car
across the Five Mile Dream
when I was 16,
my grandmother and I,
broken antennae
picking up

two stations
across 400 miles.
My grandmother is
a storyteller—
the most natural kind,
who lived a life of
detailed observation and
sharp memory,
with a keen sense
of intrigue.
My grandmother devours stories,
hungers for new plots,
new characters,
new ways to see.

She told me stories
for 400 miles
of a time I've never seen,
on shores familiar and foreign,

and I learned to measure

my life

in the telling.

I wonder often

of genetics,

the things we carry

in the blood—

if I crave words

because she does,

or because my mother

never denied me

just one more chapter

those late nights

she used to read to me.

I wonder, often

when her stories

became mine.

My grandma's bar
still has a jukebox—
I've never asked
who updates it,
songs, appearing and
disappearing
over the years like
torn leather on
booth seats,
dance floors
no one uses anymore,
worn and replaced
beneath the pool table
where I first learned
why angles matter
but even now,
a thousand miles away,
I know there's a song
on that jukebox

just waiting to be sung,

a story

waiting to be told,

and I know all the words.

Star Gazing

"We smoked cigarettes and we stared at the moon,

and I'd show you stars you never could see"

I remember

the first time

I understood

the flutter of anticipation

when I popped out the screen

of my bedroom window—

armed with a flashlight,

I crawled onto the roof

and felt almost free.

I made it a habit,

late at night,

when far as I could see,
everyone else was asleep.
I brought you with me—
I've lost count how often—
and tried to show you
the skies
through my eyes.
You'd ask me about
constellations
long before those
star-gazing apps,
a Walkman between us,
one headphone each,
a well-worn CD
spinning the songs
we'd close our eyes to,
promising our future
would hurt less
than our past.

Line Break

"I got a room at the top of the world tonight

and I ain't coming down"

The friction of

rough shingles

scraping against

bare feet

has saved me

more times than

I can count.

I'd blink up at a dark sky,

freezing rain tangling my hair,

pulling the fire and smoke

into my lungs,
the ragged breaths of tragedy
catching on the exhale.

Who were we then,
weak in our angst,
the sharp claws of loneliness
digging beneath the skin,
slowly burning us up,
suffocating towards a
break of skin
break of sky
break of a life
taken with shaking hands,
a plague in a
hopeless wasteland,
where your empty desk
became a beacon
for every wandering soul

trying to understand

why some of us

always keep fighting,

growing numb in

freezing rain

screaming at

dark skies,

no one to tell us

come down,

come inside,

it's alright,

just the voices of the dead

echoing in the margins

somewhere between

now and then.

This Is Your Song

"You speak to me in natural harmony

like we both grew up with nothin'

and I can't believe my own memory

but it one day could be coming

and I don't even know the wrong I've done

and I don't even care anymore

all I know is I believe that you and me forever

will stand accused of love."

I still have the mixtape

you made me in 8th grade.

I hadn't touched it in years,

afraid of the raw memories

preserved despite my revised retellings—

See, I never mention you now,
your presence only acknowledged
in your first real absence, like
I tell people
about my vanilla vodka breakup,
shot for shot for
every memory
I no longer wanted,
every letter you sent
up in flames.

Turns out, not even I
could erase you
from my narrative—
something about those formative years and
the ditches we crawled our way out of,
the late nights on back roads,
singing through the sunroof
like a classic 80s movie scene and

you were the only other 7th grader
who knew Stevie Nicks.

Once upon a time,
we were going to get out
of this place which claimed
so much of our hearts.
Best laid plans of
meek and disillusioned teenagers
unafraid, then, of tempting fate—
singing “I Will Survive” at the top of
our lungs, rooftops of parking structures or
wherever we remembered the words,
convinced we already knew
we’d die there too.

It’s the kind of irony
only fate could call,
far beyond the powers of

even the most talented writers—

a kind of cruel irony,

that a miracle

lasts just long enough—

and memory

doesn't seem to care

that love and hate live together

in these inner chambers,

my resentment

chaffing against

every time you saved me.

Back Roads

"Oh, yeah, you wreck me baby

you break me in two

but you move me honey,

yes you do"

I never told you,

all those years ago

as I followed you

into that warm

Midwestern summer night

when you gave me

my first cigarette—

you were already

a memory to me,

more idea

than substance,

and maybe

that's the point

of all those back roads,

the round-about ways

we always found

of never really

going anywhere.

I never told you

how I craved

your closeness,

convinced

even when you touched me

you couldn't see me at all.

We connect,

more often than not,

in half-truths,

loaded omissions—

like when I say

you still roll

the perfect joint,

I never tell you

I still daydream

—occasionally—

of your hands,

how I suspect

your fingers

would feel

running through my hair—

like long overdue

resolution

and forgiveness

I never intended

to withhold—

an accidental dawning—

the kind I stumble upon

after a late-night
book binge,
desperate for a fade out
as light crawls into the corners,
nursing a hangover
that wrings out the soul.
And I never could name
that feeling—
those late nights,
those back roads,
filled with song,
smoke, fire and
light touches
unsure, hesitant
unrecognizable
even then
unsure of what we were
we were always something.

Severe isolation
left my already tenuous
relationship with touch
at mad levels—
a madness of
between the binaries where
any touch
left me torn,
recoiling and yearning.

Suddenly, I'm reminded
of that time
you gave me
my first joint.
I think about it now,
how this one just isn't the same and
how I occasionally let you
touch me
when I didn't want you to.

I remember that time
I thought I knew
what touch-starved meant,
that night in the rain,
rain I felt coming
from hours away
and I basked in the
warm caress
of a summer downpour
but felt nothing
when your lips
touched mine.
I thought I knew
who I was
but when you're young
people who have
dimmed their brightness
tell you
this is the brightest

you will ever shine.

Whatever light I keep

somewhere in my veins,

gathers strength

in the passing of the years,

and I have grown tired

of standing still

in the growing darkness.

The streetlights are beautiful,

here, amongst an inky sky

and I will find the words

to tell you I crave

the letter game

we used to play,

spelling words, strung together by

sure fingers

tracing each symbol

one at a time

across skin.

Echo

"I promise you this winter

I will worship you like gold"

We don't talk
about old scars,
pale reminders
of darker days—
relative, always—
easy for you
not to see.
We don't talk
about what I mean
when I say these
winters are hard

like they used to be—

you scoff,

mutter something about

climate change

like monsters

will have a harder time

finding us in the slush—

but I remember

how clearly

they see in the dark.

Detour

"Yeah we were desperate then

to have each other to hold

but love is a long, long road"

When I close my eyes

summon your memory,

I still see the rain

fogged glasses discarded—

useless—

that first time

I convinced you to dance

barefoot on wet grass,

your bright laugh

in a lazy gray sky,

as I'd exaggerate
each syllable.
I knew all the lines
always already
knowing even then
we'd part ways on
awkward embraces,
promises broken
before ever spoken.
But I remember you here,
in a warm steady rain,
no heartache in sight.

I told myself
I'd never write to you
in a poem—
our ending was not
poetic, not meaningful,
beautiful or bittersweet.

The thing is,

there's nothing really to say.

We don't know each other,

not anymore, or maybe again—

like when we first met,

anonymously drawn to

words on a page,

a single voice

in a crowd of millions,

and I found yours.

I told myself

I wouldn't write

to tell you

sometimes,

I still wake up

with your voice

ringing in my ears,

and when I see

another neglected mug

collecting dust

on an overstocked nightstand—

sometimes,

I forget the 'where's and 'what's

and I think

it was you,

already gone to work,

leaving me fresh

morning coffee

just the way I like it,

without ever having to

leave the bed.

A labor of love

I still remember,

mostly because

I know

you never drank coffee.

So, this is just to say

I hope this world

has not made you hard,

when I know

how tender

your affection can be.

Driver Picks the Music

"Call out the instigator

because there's something in the air

we've got to get together sooner or later

because the revolution's here

and you know it's right

and you know that it's right"

We always talk a good game—

veer away from

dystopian futures and

imagine instead, a reality of

crumbling institutions,

a decolonized world,

listening for the death rattle

of capitalism,

like Indigenizing

the Federation of Planets

to include a 24th century

grown past the Tonto stereotypes,

because the most relatable thing

Chakotay ever said was,

"I wanna go home"

when describing an Arizona sunset.

But I check myself,

admit it might actually be

closer to the 25th,

the daily reminders that

most of my friends

can't even hear the triggers

that set me off

over the laugh tracks,

and I wonder

how a ghost

can join a revolution.

Maybe, I say,

they call this ice

in my veins

a sure sign of burnout,

when you slow down,

count the heartbeats

of everyone in the room

who locked knowing eyes,

like our pulses align

as we roll our eyes,

too tired now

to fake it.

My father always told me

"pick your battles,

you can't fight them all,"

and I wonder

if he ever bothered

to pick any worthy fights at all—
like, listening to a rant
about taxes and birth control
I tell him
I just wanna change the world,
and how long
is this revolution gonna take
if my own father
can't even get past
the past tense—
can I take a beat,
press pause on
a broken record
to point out the missing pieces?
My pulse skips with
each groove
you've forgotten was even there
like, I can't really envision
an intersectional movement

when they only see
museum quality
monstrosities,
and I know
my revolution
will never be televised,
because they still
can't get past
the past tense.

I remember the day
I told him my vision
of a world changed—
where gender was
never a binary and
sexuality was
a personal journey,
guns didn't radicalize
toxic masculinity and

I wasn't afraid

on every dark street.

He said, "you're dreamin' babe,"

and laughed

when I said

"I'm not the only one."

B Side

"I saw you sail across a river

underneath Orion's sword

in your eyes there was a freedom

I had never known before"

I made the playlist

for my mother's third wedding

four hours before

alarms would sound,

and I had places to be.

The kind of exhausted

that forbids sleep,

desperately,

I sought your voice,

and for the last time,
you read me poetry
until I fell asleep.
I told you
how surprised I was
she wanted
"The Dark of the Sun,"
that Tom Petty
reminded me of
a man she already left.
Maybe, you said,
it reminded her of me,
the same way Orion
brings me home
to sisters
reading on dark porches,
flashlights and cigarettes,
greeting winter's
brightest stars

instead of you,

half a world away.

My mother and I

bury the past

to take something back:

memory is funny that way.

I-80

"Now the good ol' days may not return

And the rocks might melt, and the sea may burn

I'm learning to fly but I ain't got wings

coming down is the hardest thing."

I often anthropomorphize time

just to check in—

we speak casually,

like just another ghost

stopping by my passenger's seat,

and I offer

the last drags of

this stretch's cigarette

to the concrete rivers

sweeping my tires along—
sometimes returning
looks a lot like leaving,
and small ceremonies
keep me grounded
along the way.
Time and I,
we have an
oddly flexible relationship, and
time has a funny way of
occasionally surprising me—
like this one time,
somewhere between
memory and prophecy,
I thought maybe
even time gets cold,
when everything froze,
but no,
it was more like a favor—

allowing my easy slide
across 3 lanes
to an exit
that was more of an escape hatch
when a loose Semi
jackknifed,
nothing but
broken glass and red lights in its wake.

And this time, I think
something must be said
about the company I keep and
promises made,
because regardless of
fate,
we skirted the edges,
caught our breaths on
shaking inhales,
in harmony,

(there in my passenger's seat)

another young deer woman

old before her time,

who always sings

old songs with me,

and if our beats

are numbered,

maybe we need

more moments

where our hearts

slow,

a secret to keep,

between us and time.

Coming down,

I recounted the story

I was told

about the seed

secured around my wrist

from a river

I've only ever dreamt about,

and the protection it gives

in the liminal spaces,

between here and there

or somewhere else entirely—

Time just laughed

as I lit another cigarette,

a *liohbwana* in every exhale,

grateful for

small ceremonies,

small stories and

old familiar songs.

Powwow Mixtape

"A red winged hawk is circling

the blacktop stretches out for days

how could I get so close to you

and still feel so far away?

I hear a voice come on the wind

Sayin' you and I will meet again."

Every year at powwow,

we'd sneak out the back doors,

watch the skies

from the parking lot,

and without fail

we'd visit with those

familiar birds of prayer,

catching up on

the years in-between,

and I think of her now,

alone along an

unfamiliar stretch of

a highway I know well.

I think of her voice,

when last we prayed,

sweetgrass filling the front seat,

reminding me

I'm expected home again—

with a heavy sign and

a heavy foot on the gas,

I push forward,

hours, miles, or

kilometers, or

whatever arbitrary assignment of

distance.

I measure all things

in time—

like how many songs

until I can stop for the night,

relying on

couch surfing in the diaspora,

grateful I'm not alone in

even my own displacement

even when I lose sleep

in lieu of telling stories,

like the physical reminder

of each other

brings every memory

back to the surface,

and can you believe

what a year it's been?

Twelve moons waxing and waning and

is it just me

or does every year

feel more like a dare,

fate and survivance

taking bets

on which exit

gets us there quicker.

American Girl

"raised on promises

she couldn't help thinkin' that there

was a little more life

somewhere else"

Morning's burning

sage

lingers

in the threads

of a sweater too thin.

Ceremony lingers,

well-past closing.

Midnight,

a dark parking lot,

we played our Snapchats

of drum circles,

one dancing,

one singing.

In a world of our own,

we celebrated our births,

you, remembering

fancy-dancing,

me, singing

“American Girl”

because I never learned

the dance,

but I could shape these words

to match the beat.

Between cigarettes and sweetgrass

and the heartbeat

of ceremony drums,

we'd quote Smoke Signals

from memory

contemplate absence
of fathers,
forgiveness,
and forgetting.

My grandfather was a truck driver
for over 40 years and
I wonder how many
of his favorite songs
I sing to on long drives,
and does he sing with me?
Sometimes, I like to think
he takes these opportunities
to get to know me.
I can't help but feel him
when the sun slants just right,
long shadows on a
long winter road and I
count the turns to home.

It's important,

on long lonely drives,

to have a good copilot

playing DJ.

I wonder what stories

my grandpa told

late at night

on a CB radio.

Sometimes I think

had I been a stranger

I could've known him better.

Most days I'm just

a well-worded contradiction,

knowing I'm missing

more than I know,

wondering why you're here

more often as a ghost

than you ever were alive.

Miles to Burn

"Last dance with Mary Jane,

one more time to kill the pain

I feel summer creepin' in and I'm

tired of this town again."

I told them once

about this quote

from N. Scott Momaday,

something about

an old love of going,

returning like

the restlessness

bubbling beneath my skin

is just as cyclical

as anything else.
"I'm not Kiowa,"
I tell them,
because Momaday was very specific,
but I get it.
Something always finds
a way
to draw me west like
chasing a setting sun,
retracing steps
of ghosts.
It's not that I'm tired,
I tell them,
not of the water,
or the forests—
impressive, still,
even massacred
as they were
by an industry

who considers them
exploitable—
when the world ends,
these waters
will be the last of us.
I'm not tired
of the magic here, but
I'm tired of
fighting the winter
and monsters
who stalk
every familiar alley
and I wonder
what life would be like
if I weren't so consistently
preparing for disaster,
the steps we take
to convince ourselves we're safe—
or something close,

with a flashlight, pepper spray or
whatever else they
tell you can save you, but,
fire is the only cure
I've ever seen work,
and all those old trees
are burning in the west—
I'm not tired,
I tell them,
I'm just restless
waiting on the world
our parents promised.

And yet,
when I embrace my
longing of going,
those long stretches of
Midwest trees passing by
brings me back,

always,

to those warm summer nights,

counting fireflies,

(fewer than

when we were kids,

armed with mason jars),

pews placed precariously around

whatever we've wrangled

to burn through the night,

our brightest dreams and

most bitter rants

equally exchanged

in the early and

late hours.

I still laugh, recalling

when we learned

first-hand

how fast

a mattress goes up in flames,

and the heat

piercing the dark

still warms my mind,

grounds me,

no matter where I drift.

Night Driver

"There's a shadow on the moon tonight

I swear I see your face

up there with the satellites

looking down from outer space.

Me, I'm drifting home again

headlights in my eyes

fighting sleep with windows down

worn out from long goodbyes."

Alone, counting headlights

on a dark highway

with windows down,

trying to convince

cooler air

to keep me

between the lines,

sometimes, it feels like

all I do is leave—

parting words echo

on the other side of

returning,

like belonging nowhere, but

always missing someone,

somewhere.

I prefer the passenger's seat

on dark empty streets,

be it back roads or

highways,

playing DJ,

keeping track of the moon, but

when it's just

me and a familiar playlist,

I find, sometimes,
space enough to reflect on
why goodbyes have become
such a sharp focus—
I've learned
too many times
you never think
it'll be the last.
I hear death
just around the bend,
and I can't get
that distracting attempt
of living
out of my ear,
or Dickinson
out of my head—
because I could not stop for death.
I could not stop for death,
only pause to mourn–

alone in elevators,
when breaths catch,
hook themselves on tears
and lungs squeeze shut
holding them in,
or behind the wheel
when sudden wrenching
forces a side-road stop,
and how to explain
to kind strangers
being stranded by
heartbreak
is so much harder
than a flat tire.

And I can't say
whether or not
you felt my fingers
in your hair,

my hand

on your forehead—

or if the eyes

are windows to the soul,

what does it mean

when they become mirrors,

a rippled reflection

of nothing more

than my own grief and

finally

I understand

the breakdown of the binary—

like sometimes letting go

is the only way

to hold on.

I-94

"We grew up fast

and no one seemed to notice

we grew up fast

and we grew up alone."

A setting summer sun

highlighting the

Detroit skyline

is my only company

on this journey home

and I think of you.

I don't miss the misery

of our inseparable years,

railing against

a world unforgiving

in the dark hours

of our youth.

What I miss

is the comfort

of our silence,

an understanding

of all we survived

never needing

validation

and the brightness

you bring

to the corners

of a dark vision.

It still amazes me,

sometimes,

that after all these years

you're still the one

most familiar

with the dark truths of
who I was,
occasionally
still am—
like a wrong turn down
memory lane
leading back to
dark roads
we never should have been on,
margins scattered with
broken glass we'd
try to ignore
bitter nights,
long winter shadows
creeping far too early
and we used to get so lost—
it's still a joke,
my talent for
always finding a way home,

the origins obscured
by the secrets we kept of
moonless summer nights
on unfamiliar streets
trying to run away
and get home
at the same time.

I think of her still, sometimes,
sleeping in my passenger's seat,
what I gave to indulge her
"only the good die young" attempts to
cheat death,
and as she slept,
I learned to listen
to the whisper on a
highway wind,
one only I could hear
winding back down

dirt roads,

and I'm still grateful

for the lessons I learned early

about listening

even if no one else

can hear.

Feeding the Fire

"you can live on nothing at all

and I ain't gonna be

hungry no more"

There are days

when nothing really happens at all—

I count my breaths

just to do something,

close my eyes

listen for the wind,

the quiet music

of rustling leaves

and I think

if I could time travel

I'd hang out often
in a slower-paced time,
if such a thing
ever really existed,
like when we'd visit
and speak
with the intention
of a journey,
because the truth is,
the constant grind
of these trying times
is burning out the
brightest flames
in everyone I love,
and spending a day
just being
brings all the baggage of
our slow-burn apocalypse,
crippling anxiety of

never having done

enough.

There are days

when I wonder

if I can truly forgive

the generations before me

for their silence,

complicity

belligerent adherence to

living by

stealing from descendants,

believing

it'd never catch up to them.

In the midst of

mass extinction,

my mother tells me

she also wonders

at her generation,

when they lost

their fire for justice,

when they put aside

their desire

for a better world

and settled for

a life unexamined, or

I guess sometimes,

surviving,

instead of revolution,

but the cycles of time

keep compounding,

ancient monsters

still stalking,

and not talking

about monsters

doesn't mean

they disappear,

I'd much rather

shine a light

than fear the dark.

So to feed the fire

inside my veins

I gave up

settling.

Red River

for Tina Fontaine,
and all MMIWG2S

"So meet me tonight by the Red River

where the water is clear and cold

meet me tonight by the Red River

and look down into your soul"

There's a unique quiet

alone on a frozen river

in the setting sun—

winter's long shadows

echo

with my breath,

the long fingers of

winter's hungry monsters
creeping from trees
on the shore's edge,
waiting to feast
on forgotten bodies below.
The ice moans
with each step
and I wonder—
with so many lost
in a watery grave
of colonial indifference—
if I've taken
any step forward at all.
I can't find peace here,
nor rest
where ghosts linger
waiting for justice
that will never come.
The soul of a nation

reflected here,

in this frozen river—

cold, muddy

—guilty.

Between a Memory and a Dream

"But let's get to the point,

let's roll another joint

and turn the radio loud,

I'm too alone to be proud"

Insomnia

is a funny thing.

My favorite time to write

has always been

the quiet moments

between consciousness

and sleep

or the moments before waking

desperately holding on

to whatever my tired mind
uses to calm my thoughts.

I call it
moonlight baking
when insomnia drives
mad experimentation.
Dancing with ghosts
in the kitchen,
music plays
loud enough
to drown out memory,
and time
seems to slow
twirling like smoke
between the sleeping world
and where I find myself
somewhere in the dark.
Voices from margins

of my own narratives

comfort,

in the same old ways.

We understand each other,

always,

across time.

Belong

"You belong among the wildflowers,

you belong in a boat out at sea.

Sail away, kill off the hours,

you belong somewhere you feel free"

The diaspora is large,

and I have been

a stranger

in every home

I've ever known.

A constant visitor

amongst the expanse

of inland seas,

of childhood memory,

a water that comforts,
and soothes—
and here,
in this cold prairie,
whose muddy waters
speak to me
of hopeless isolation.
Belonging seems
(in pieces)
a word
of contradictions—
to be longing
the opposite
of what I imagine
it feels to belong.
On these bright days,
melting ice, drifting
through dark, sparkling water,
I feel longing,

the constant pull
of desert flowers—
a river
that bears the name,
the first word
I learned to spell.
"You are
Y-A-Q-U-I,"
and a story
my mother used to tell
before turning out the lights,
repeating the words
her father taught her:
"—don't ever tell,
but don't ever forget."

Past, present, future
collide, here
in this moment of

quiet rivers—

the words

that will always

carry me home.

Record Store Rarities

for Jack

"And if I never do nothin'

I'm coming back someday

'cause you got a heart so big

it could crush this town

and I can't hold out forever

even walls fall down"

I tried to write

a love letter

to Winnipeg,

to living on

another river

farther from the one

I dream of,

and I remember

watching the thunder

roll across the prairie.

I remember

letting the sky

light up the room,

and you.

Sometimes we're lucky enough

to be listening

when that voice says

"this one is special"—

a compulsion to

dig a little deeper,

take a chance on a

rare find.

You appeared suddenly

a new constant,

as natural as gravity—

and I realized

this city

(through your eyes)

can almost

be like home.

You brought me Redbone

and Buffy Sainte-Marie

with morning coffee,

filled my days

with familiar old words,

and nights with song,

and art and whiskey,

binging Netflix and beading

into the late hours,

always laughing

at the same jokes,

quoting the same

old movies we'd memorized

so long ago.

And I never wanted
to miss this place—
but the stubborn prairie
offered me
a new kind of survival,
lessons in remembering
even here,
in these biting winds—
amongst the many
invisible knives
slicing across
my skin, my voice,
my spirit—
there is warmth.

An Interlude

for Lori

"Well I know what's right

I got just one life.

In a world that keeps on pushin' me around

but I'll stand my ground

and I won't back down."

An early birthday present,

she tells me

and I don't know why

I'm still surprised

she always remembers,

hands me a piece

of my childhood

from a story I once told.

I don't know how to tell her
she constantly reminds me
of endless strength,
of the powerful women
I often find myself
surrounded by,
awkward in my gratitude,
unaccustomed to
such thoughtful gestures.

When I drive
towards a spring sunset
I wonder at my luck,
and when she emails
to tell me
a deer stopped
to follow
my taillights
as she watched me leave,

I want to tell her

about ceremonies

and prophecy,

to thank her

for the warning

she didn't know

she was giving me.

Instead,

I offer her

my favorite deer story.

Road Music

"People are what people make 'em,

and that ain't gonna change.

There ain't nothin' you can do,

nothing you could rearrange

but I forgive it all

I forgive it all."

There's something about

California highways—

the valleys and the mountains—

unique to this place

where I often confuse

reality and myth.

Story dominates

what I know of this

valley of my dead,

witness to generations

of our songs

and I often wonder

what my grandfather sang

to these highways

I only ever remember

for what I've lost.

They say gratitude

changes the patterns

in your brain,

like reprogramming

the presets after

returning home

to new stations

instead of old friends

and my mother asks me

—did anything good

happen today?

But I remember

her speechless,

her anger in grief

just like mine

and I try

to let go

move towards gratitude

as fast as she does.

I wonder

what makes my mother

a storyteller

and not a poet—

why I so often

speak to ghosts

as she tells stories—

and I wonder

if she sees

the same pain

I hear in these rhythmic valleys,

as the sun beats down

and I drum again

against the steering wheel,

listening for

another memory.

Of Desert Highways

"love isn't easy

isn't always kind

but I could have stood there

lost in your eyes"

"There's a story there—"

It wasn't a question,

but an observation

that brought me back

to poetry.

I told her

of the Apache artist

whose vision I saw

on instinct

that sunny afternoon
when I married the mountain—
omitted in the retelling
the mountain that sang to me
that time in the desert,
that moment I return
over and over again
trying to find the words
to the song my blood
dances to,
steady and sure of every step—
I didn't tell her
that I admire
the quiet genius
of her seeing,
that I couldn't tell her
what it meant to go home
to a home I've missed
all my life

to return

to the land my ghosts remember

without exposing

the darkest parts of me,

and all I wanted

was to tell her

a good story.

She was a deer woman,

piercing with a

generous gaze,

promising a return

the journey back

from the land of the dead

but deer woman never needed

the song of a man

to find her way,

not that Eurydice

ever had a say.

My people say

the men always call

to the deer,

dancing, singing, hunting,

but my favorite story

was always

the deer who never played the game,

who lived, witnessed,

and died

on its own terms—

invisible, they called it,

and I know

sometimes being invisible

is the only way to survive, but,

it's impossible to explain

if you don't already know

the ways invisibility

can save your life.

Uncommon Mapping

"Don't be afraid to live what you believe

nothin' matters

(it doesn't matter)

when you keep a little soul

nothing really matters anymore"

Once again

I find myself

opening Holy Week

driving down

a southwest highway

singing to my dead.

I often tell people

I have a

strange relationship
with California,
leave it with a
"I've got family out there,"
between those valleys and mountains,
this place
so much of my family
called home
for so long,
and what is more
American
than a California highway?
And what confluence
of Tricksters
led me through
another valley in
some kind of shade
like manifesting the
stainless glass scene of

a valley I memorized

as a child

in the shadow of death,

singing the same songs

when I promised myself

never again

would I impress a priest.

I think about Alcatraz

as I light a cigarette

at a gas station in Oakland.

A woman gestures her way

into offering a trade:

her coins for my tobacco,

but I know better:

tobacco is always

a gift

and a prayer

and I let

small gestures

take pieces of my anger.

I think of Trudell

as I exhale,

and the truth of power—

when I was a kid,

long before I found his music,

I'd hear stories of

a man so eloquent

his words evoked power

within "the Indians of all tribes"

a rekindling of

ancient fires so fierce,

he was feared,

but I knew

he understood me

when he said poetry

saved his life.

I heard stories of
The Spokesman of Alcatraz,
a legend of revolution,
who taught me
it's okay to demand better.
I remember touching
the writing scrawled
on the arch at Wounded Knee,
dates I'd committed to memory,
reminders of massacres and
why the ghosts hang so heavy.
I remember
closing my eyes
and knowing
his spirit is still there, too,
wherever else he might be,
that our memory is long
and deep
and we belong

to an ancient power,

its purest manifestation

igniting within

the blood of survivors—

and isn't that memory

just another kind of

survivance—

finding gratitude

through echoes

of ancestors,

and the tricks

my ghosts like to play.

Almost Home

"We were caught up in a barroom fight

'til an Indian shot out the lights.

I'm so tired of being tired,

as sure as night will follow day

most things I worry about

never happen anyway"

The thing about storytellers—

they never tell

the same story twice,

not really, 'cause

the cadence changes

with each breath and

even practiced phrases

are heard with

different ears and

sometimes I wonder

what it is

about words strung together

in precise, often clumsy

strings of sounds, and

what do we lose

in a story never heard?

When I was young

my mother told me

about bounties—

the body unwanted,

reduced to a fraction—

a head, a scalp, an ear, a

life lost for

much less than 30 pieces of silver

but these days

I think

bounties are harder to see,
revealed instead,
the payment rests
in the freedom to
walk away
and I wonder
at the nature of things,
time and its echoing themes
as I bury my kin,
the missing indicative of
the anger I cannot abandon—
I don't know what to do
with the pressure building
beneath my chest,
difficult to swallow
words leaking out
like water
that just keeps flowing
in monsoon season,

little rivers
like veins
down concrete
and I know
you can flow
to the river
just this side of home,
that place we're always
trying to get back.
Wikipedia says survivor's guilt
is a manifestation of PTSD,
and I wonder if that's why
I Google the 44-year-old man
who slammed into my cousin's car,
his life stolen on
a California road for
seconds of someone else's
easy distraction and
I don't think it's survivor's guilt

fueling my rage.

He told me once,

he couldn't ever

be drafted, he said

he was the only one

who could carry

our family name,

they couldn't make us

disappear—

not that way—

but maybe,

my family has been

running

for so long

because stories of

returning home

only end

in tragedy.

Regardless,

somehow,

I too, always

crawl back to you.

To Tom:

"I threw all I had

into the sea,

now I want a little back,

this one's for me."

I wish I could tell you

how many times

you saved my life, but

somehow, I think

you already know.

My life rides

the rhythm of your voice,

memories embodied in

every song,

the most constant presence

I've ever known,

and the only man

who always knew

just what to say.

Everyone who rides in

my passenger's seat knows

my own twist on

rules of the road:

no one changes the station

when Tom Petty sings.

LINER NOTES

The First Song

I don't remember the first time I visited California. I was too young and too sick to form many lasting memories—instead I have snapshots and fleeting scenes with no context. The first time I remember visiting California, it was my 10th birthday. An occasional and unfortunate reality of Aries babies is that every few years our birthdays may fall on Easter, or Good Friday, or some other early-spring-related religious event. This happened a few times in my life (so far), but when I turned 10, it was Easter Sunday and we were on our way to visit my father's 'religious-enough-for-Easter-brunch' side of the family. When I saw the exit sign for Ventura Boulevard, the lines "move west down Ventura Boulevard/ and all the bad boys are standing in the shadows/ and the good girls are home with broken hearts" ran through my head on a loop. The joke referenced in the poem was always something along the lines of, "you must have been the only baby who knew all the words to 'Free Fallin'" or "you came out of the womb singing that song." It's a typical dad joke I suppose, but I'll never forget when my father didn't realize he was making it on my birthday. My sister did though—and her joke was actually funny.

Driving Lessons

It can be difficult to tell sometimes if dwelling in a particular memory is optimistic or masochistic. Sometimes it's both. Most people adore my father—they think he's funny, personable, probably handsome. And there are many things I loved about my father. But I also know he was toxic to me in many ways, and often imparted the wrong lessons. He spoke often but rarely listened, and he never admitted to mistakes. The truth is my father was a terrible teacher, and while I absolutely drum on my steering wheel, I do not tailgate. I kept the driving lessons from my mother instead; while also playful, she was consistent in modeling and voicing a defensive approach (with the exception of what she calls Tiger Stadium Mode).

In the opening of "Runnin' Down a Dream"—the song referenced in the poem and one of my father's favorites—Tom sings, "I had the radio on, I was driving/ trees flew by, me and Del were singing, 'little runaway'" (lines 2-3). Del Shannon's "Runaway" is a song that topped the charts when my mother was a year old. I find it fascinating for how upbeat and joyous it sounds despite the melancholic quality of the lyrics. In the song, Del seems to wonder why he finds himself miserable and alone, with no real answers as to why the woman he loved left, or where she went. It's very clearly a lament for being left behind. I can't say I've met very many people in my life with the name Del, so it shouldn't be surprising that my mother recalls her father's old friend with the same name.

Associations can be that simple for my mother. But, I know that my grandfather returned to California when he left my mother's family, and I can't help but wonder if—feeling the subtle lament in these songs—she thinks of her father for the same reasons I think of mine.

Deer Crossing

What I appreciated most about my linguistics classes and early literary theory classes was the way they taught me to understand the flexibility of symbols and meaning. I wrote a paper once as an undergraduate about Coleridge making up symbolism completely out of nowhere; in "The Rhyme of the Ancient Mariner," Coleridge uses an albatross to carry changing meaning throughout the story. By the end, it comes to represent a great burden, and that meaning has carried through in our culture now for centuries. And it wasn't just the Romantics. Symbols are culturally specific as well; what can represent a dream in one culture can represent death in another. The symbolism of a deer is going to change depending on who you ask (even between Indigenous cultures across Turtle Island), and I think the flexibility is beautiful.

My uncle once told me that many of our trails and roads were created by following deer tracks. I never asked where he learned that information because it seemed obvious to me; walking through the woods as much as I did, following the deer tracks always proved the wisest course.

Road Trip

There's a place in the Upper Peninsula of Michigan (what we lovingly refer to as the UP) called the Keweenaw. From the middle of the lower peninsula, it's approximately 400 miles through some of the most beautiful wooded roads I've ever seen. And because we measure distance in hours and not miles, I should add that it's an average of 16 hours. I made this trip with my grandmother multiple times over the years, and not once did we have a well-working radio until the year I turned 30. "The Five Mile Dream" is what we call the Mackinac Bridge that connects Michigan's lower and upper peninsulas.

My family often jokes that we're "bad at feelings." Mostly, this means there are many things we don't say but somehow imply. My grandmother didn't say how much she loved us, but she always brought our favorite food. I suppose these were early lessons in subtext.

Star Gazing

When I was young, it was a constant game to find places that felt like freedom. I broke many rules doing so, some more egregious than others. But sitting on the roof late at night was a favorite sin of mine, and it became a place where I was free to feel openly and completely. I will never forget it, and I often miss it.

Line Break

Just after my tenth birthday, I read in *Rolling Stone* that Tom Petty and The Heartbreakers were releasing a new album titled *Echo*, and the day it was released, I pestered my father into taking me to the nearest record store so I could get it. He handed me a twenty and said he'd wait in the car, so I went in and asked the first clerk I could find where the newest Tom Petty album would be. Bless the late GenXers and the earliest of the Millennials for their constant refusal to acknowledge parental advisory warnings—that young man led me right to it, although wearing a perplexed expression the entire time, and rang me up with only the question, "how did someone your age get into Tom Petty?" It's a question I've never stopped answering.

I couldn't have known then how important this album would become for me. Nowhere near the success of *Full Moon Fever, Echo* topped out the charts at 10th place, but it became a go-to for me in the most desperate times of my young teenage years, trapped in survival mode with no means of understanding what that even meant. The overall tone of the album is quite melancholic (in my mind at least) and it was soothing to me like nothing else, when everything else was raging. Even now, it's the first album I search for when my grief feels fresh.

In the first year of my master's degree, I was a TA for a woman with a reputation for being intense and polarizing. She taught African American Literature, and I learned a great deal from her, but there was one conversation I will never forget: it was the shortest conversation of that kind I'd ever had. She asked me where I went to high school—small though my town was, it was just down the road, so she knew immediately when I told her the name. She looked me directly in the eyes, put her hand on my shoulder and told me my survival was a miracle. It was a kind of validation I'd never before received, and it offered me a new way to heal while still remembering. I haven't forgotten the people who did not make it out of my high school alive, although I rarely speak their names anymore.

This is Your Song

Once upon a time, I had a friend who—knowing my love of Tom Petty—included her favorite Tom Petty song on a mixed CD she burned for me. It was, "Stand Accused of Love" and ever since, the song has reminded me of her. She was one of my best friends, and my worst break-up. She died halfway through her 30th year, and because we were all from a small town, I heard the news shortly after the fact. I could have made it to her funeral, but I didn't go—I wrote this instead.

Back Roads

Most people who know me have heard my favorite "fun fact" about Carly Simon's cleverness regarding "You're So Vain." I read an interview with her once, many years ago, where she admits that each stanza is about a different man, and I think that's just beautiful. She was undeniably an influence in writing this poem.

I wrote this poem in Winnipeg, a city that taught me new lessons in isolation and survival. I'd never gone so long without intentional, casual physical contact, and I was unprepared for the emotional turmoil this absence would cause. Retrospectively, after the global pandemic of 2020, I'm grateful for the practice. I've thought a lot about touch in recent years; the social conceptual, psychological, and personal, and how my relationships with these things have changed over time.

Echo

The worst part of winter in Michigan is not the cold—it's that there is so little sunlight, it's easy to become depressed. The cold isn't fun, but it isn't as unbearable as other places. When I was young, I was drawn to the Ojibwe stories of the Wendigo—a giant cannibal monster of the winter. To be honest, I was drawn to the horror/monster genre in general, but Wendigo stuck with me in ways most others did not. I was fascinated by the idea that there were seasonal monsters, because winter had a habit of bringing out the monstrous in me. Depression—seasonal or not—is not easy to talk about. I find it's difficult for anyone to conceptualize if they haven't experienced it, and for those trying so hard to reach out and connect, deflection and dismissal can feel like a betrayal. When I first heard the lines from "Echo" used to open this poem, I thought to myself, "clearly someone actually gets it." Sometimes people need extra care in the dark seasons. The song also very clearly references heroin use, and this too was a problem of epidemic proportions as I was growing up, alongside fentanyl, opioids, and whip-its. It's a song that comforted me in the times I felt hopeless, if only because I felt less alone in it.

Detour

So, this is just to say:

I know I referenced William Carlos Williams in this poem, but really, it's the opposite of selfishly eating someone's plums that they were trying to save.

Driver Picks the Music

For as long as I can remember, driving represented a certain kind of freedom that I could not wait to embrace. I started as soon as I possibly could, and got my license about a week after my 16th birthday in April, 2005. What initially started as veto power soon established itself as clear Rules of the Road, the beginnings of which were formed in the years of riding along with my mom, where shotgun reads off album titles until the driver goes, "yes, that one!" Ultimately, it came down to one truth: the driver picks the music.

The September after I got my license, *Supernatural* ran its pilot episode, "Jericho," and for the first time, I heard Dean Winchester say, "Driver picks the music, shotgun shuts his cakehole." I resonated quickly with this character who shared both my driving rules and more of my musical influences than my peers, and the show filled a void in me left by *X-Files* and *Buffy*. It's safe to say it was a major influence on me over the years, alongside the many other multi-year fandoms I've participated in, and this poem is absolutely riddled with nerd references. There's even a *Star Trek: Voyager* reference, which I will always publicly admit to being the worst of any Star Trek series. All of this to say, I'm grateful to these worlds for the practice in imaging beyond an apocalypse.

B Side

Weddings are exhausting. And my mother did that three times. I was only present for the third myself. While I managed very little sleep that night, at least I was awake in the comfort of my own home. My sister had to drive all through the night to make it home in time.

I-80

When I tell people this story, I usually start it off with, "that time Iowa tried to kill me." There are details that come and go when the story is told, but there's not usually room in the telling for the little things poetry makes space for. The seed mentioned here is called Ojo de Maso (deer eye), and it is often beaded onto personal accessories by the Yaqui who believe it protects the carrier from harm while traveling. Liohbwana is an expression of gratitude in the Yoeme language.

Powwow Mixtape

Some relationships in my life are tied to specific cycles—there are people I only ever see on the journey between places, and some I only see at recurring events. Rarely speaking outside of these episodic visits, we tend to pack all the feeling of the time missed into whatever limited hours we have.

American Girl

There are countless reasons as to why Found Family can become a powerfully important concept for people, just as there are countless reasons why we might choose someone to be our family. I made many of my closest connections by bonding through the shared experiences of the Indigenous diaspora—both the joys and the traumas. There's a multilayered understanding there that can be difficult to translate.

This poem is for Amber; it was once again my birthday, and that year it coincided with powwow.

Miles to Burn

The full quote from N. Scott Momaday is, "The Kiowa are a summer people; they abide the cold and keep to themselves, but when the season turns and the land becomes warm and vital they cannot hold still; an old love of going returns upon them." The poem speaks to the need to wander, roam, or venture—and the conflicting emotions of nostalgia and homesickness that creep in almost immediately upon leaving. This poem is for Adam, one of my obvious soulmates; thank you for all your understanding, your trust, and all the hours of deep meaning. Thank you for always being my reader, even for the ones the world will never see.

Night Driver

Grief and trauma can affect people in countless ways, and somewhere along the way, one of mine translated into a sensitivity to partings, or how I say goodbye. While almost anyone can claim that death comes unexpectedly, I'm hyper-aware of this reality, and have been for many years.

I-94

When I was first learning to drive, it was difficult for me to fully conceptualize how long interstate freeways are. I got lost many times, and usually with the same company. These adventures became my early stories, the ones we spoke in hushed tones where our parents wouldn't overhear.

Feeding the Fire

I suppose by now it might be obvious, but I like layered meaning. 'Settle' here is used in a context that speaks not only to the phenomenon of giving up the hope for something better, but also the entirety of a world created by settler-colonialism. Refusing to settle (or live according to settler-colonial rules) was a revelation for me that changed how I lived my life in countless ways.

This poem is also about exhaustion. Burnout is a terrible feeling and the reason I hear most often as to why people quit fighting for whatever it is they want to see in the world.

Red River

I don't know which Red River Tom was talking about when he wrote the song, but the one I know is not a clear one—it is brown, muddy, and always cold. I have never known cold quite like Winnipeg cold, and I have never in my life met a sadder river than the Red. Tina was, of course, far from the only person whose body was pulled from that river. There is an epidemic of missing and murdered Indigenous women, girls, and two-spirit kin, and although Tina was what some have described as a "model victim," Canadian courts declared a not-guilty verdict for the man who wrapped her body in a duvet and tossed her in the river, and justice was once again nowhere to be found.

Between a Memory and a Dream

It was a hard call on this one between "You Don't Know How It Feels" and "The Apartment Song," because of how often I must have annoyed my apartment neighbors with my loud music and singing at awkward hours of the late night/early morning.

Belong

One thing I will always be grateful to my mother for—she never told me I had to hide. She took me to powwow when I was too young to remember everything, and she has never discouraged me from the long road of reclamation. When I was a kid, she was the reason I could challenge my history teachers. She gave me biographies of Sacagawea and Crazy Horse, while the kids in my class read about Einstein and Neil Armstrong.

Record Store Rarities

What is there to say about two Indigenous US expats hanging out in Winnipeg? The best used record store we found there was unquestionably in the North End.

An Interlude

For the Yaqui people, the deer are special for their ability to move feely between our world, and Sea An'a—the Flower World, where all the dead reside. Because of this, I have long associated the deer with various aspects of the world of the dead, or the dying. They are constant reminders for me of true power. They first demonstrated for me a notion that life and death don't have to be binaries.

As stated, this poem was written for Lori, who always remembers my birthday. I shouldn't be surprised, because she is extremely gifted in memory and is a deeply thoughtful person. The moment of this gift conflates for me between life, death, and rebirth—but it was a moment of gratitude that sustained me in the days to come. I call this poem an interlude, because the memory feels like coming up for air before diving into some unfathomable depths. I began it with the words from "I Won't Back Down" because it's a memory that reminds me survival on my own terms is worth everything.

Road Music

I don't like to hold grudges, but I have a long memory, and I tend to feel things very deeply. My mother modeled extraordinary grace in grief throughout my life, but I never could cope as easily with this world as she seems to. My mother is a gifted storyteller, and people hang onto her words with rapt attention; I've listened to her stories my whole life, and over the years, I understood story as a function of living memory. I think my mom often works through her grief this way, but I needed the loaded empty spaces, layers, subtext, and rule-breaking that only poetry offered to work through my grief.

Of Desert Highways

I've heard the argument that lyric poetry begins in the tradition of Orpheus. Formal education tends to dictate one be familiar with the classics, and as a child I loved Greek mythology, so I knew the story of Orpheus early on, but he never seemed like much of a hero to me. Seriously, all the guy had to do was trust Eurydice (which he couldn't do), but no one even bothered asking if she wanted to go back with him or not, and I think that's bullshit.

Uncommon Mapping

Holy Week is, I'm told, the entire week leading into Easter Sunday. For the Yaqui, who have been heavily influenced by Catholic colonizers, this usually involves performing the Deer Dance ceremony, which tends brings a great deal of tourism to Tucson ever year. Before Catholic and Christian missionaries invaded these communities, the Deer Dance was held in the Spring. I've never seen the Deer Dance performed; there are many protocols around this ceremony, including a ban on recording devices, and every time I visit, I seem to just miss it.

I memorized Psalm 23 when I was a kid. I have no idea why—maybe I thought it was beautiful. I didn't go to church, so how I was exposed to it in its entirety is another unanswerable question, but it's certainly a popular verse at funerals. I recited it alongside the priest during the service of my aunt's funeral when I was seven years old, and he noticed. I remember him telling me how impressed he was, and how he was so sure it was a calling from god to me, specifically. I wrote off the entirety of organized religion in that moment.

Almost Home

This poem is about my cousin, who was born a week before me. He was a fun guy, full of vivacious energy with a playful spirit. I love him more than I can say, and despite the physical distance often limiting our relationship to episodic visits, I think we understood each other well. I sometimes considered him my other half, the opposite of me in so many important ways.

In the police report filed at the scene of his death, the driver who killed him admits to the cop—unprompted—that he was distracted by a porn video when he veered across the double yellow lines. My cousin died days after his 30th birthday (and days before mine).

This poem is about my cousin, and it is also about the land. There is only one direct address, and it comes at the very end; the only one who knows my cousin's whole story is the land who watched him live it, and I will always have more questions than answers.

To Tom:

Nothing but a dedication,
and endless gratitude.

REFERENCES

[1] "I'm gonna leave this world for a while"
-Tom Petty, "Free Fallin'," Full Moon Fever, 1989

[2] "runnin' down a dream/ that never would come to me/ workin' on a mystery/ goin' wherever it leads"
-Tom Petty, "Runnin' Down A Dream," Full Moon Fever, 1989

[3] "Real love is a man's salvation/ the weak ones fall/ the strong carry on"
-Tom Petty and the Heartbreakers, "Straight Into Darkness," Long After Dark, 1982

[4] "I was born with something down inside of me/ And it's carried me over, delivered me/ Yeah delivered me, I'm standing at your gate/ Just out of reach of the hands of fate"
-Tom Petty, "Deliver Me," Long After Dark, 1982

[5] "We smoked cigarettes and we stared at the moon / and I'd show you stars you never could see"
-Tom Petty, "Even the Losers," Damn the Torpedoes, 1979

[6] "I got a room at the top of the world tonight / and I ain't coming down"
-Tom Petty, "Room at the Top," Echo, 1999

[7] "You speak to me in natural harmony/ like we both grew up with nothing/ and I can't believe my own memory/ but it one day could be coming./ And I don't even know the wrong I've done/ and I don't even care anymore/ all I know is I believe that you and me/ forever will stand accused of love."
-Tom Petty, "Accused of Love," Echo, 1999

[8] "You wreck me, baby/ yeah, you break me in two/ but you move me, honey/ yes, you do"
-Tom Petty, "You Wreck Me," Wildflowers, 1994

[9] "I promise you this winter / I will worship you like gold"
-Tom Petty, "Echo," Echo, 1999

[10] "Yeah we were desperate then / to have each other to hold / but love is a long, long road"
-Tom Petty, "Love is a Long Road," Full Moon Fever, 1989

[11] "Call out the instigator/ because there's something in the air/ we've got to get together sooner or later/ because the revolution's here/ and you know it's right/ and you know that it's right"
-Tom Petty, "Something in the Air," Tom Petty and the Heartbreakers: Greatest Hits, 1993

[12] "I saw you sail across a river / Underneath Orion's sword / in your eyes there was a freedom / I had never known before"
-Tom Petty, "The Dark of the Sun," Into the Great Wide Open, 1991

[13] "Now the good ol' days may not return/ And the rocks might melt, and the sea may burn/ I'm learning to fly but I ain't got wings/ coming down is the hardest thing."
-Tom Petty, "Learning to Fly," Into the Great Wide Open, 1991

[14] "A red winged hawk is circling/ the blacktop stretches out for days/ how could I get so close to you/ and still feel so far away?/ I hear a voice come on the wind/ Sayin' you and I will meet again."
-Tom Petty, "You and I Will Meet Again," Into the Great Wide Open, 1991

[15] "raised on promises / she couldn't help thinkin' that there / was a little more life / somewhere else"
-Tom Petty, "American Girl," Tom Petty and the Heartbreakers, 1976

[16] "Last dance with Mary Jane,/ one more time to kill the pain/ I feel summer creepin' in and I'm
tired of this town again."
-Tom Petty, "Mary Jane's Last Dance," Tom Petty and the Heartbreakers: Greatest Hits, 1993

[17] "There's a shadow on the moon tonight/ I swear I see your face up there with the satellites/ looking down from outer space./ Me, I'm drifting home again/ headlights in my eyes/ fighting sleep with windows down/ worn out from long goodbyes."
-Tom Petty, "Night Driver," Highway Companion, 2006

[18] "We grew up fast/ and no one seemed to notice/ we grew up fast/ and we grew up alone."
-Tom Petty, "Grew Up Fast," She's the One, 1996

[19] "you can live on nothing at all/ and I ain't gonna be/ hungry no more"
-Tom Petty, "Hungry No More," 2 (Mudcrutch), 2016

[20] "So meet me tonight by the Red River/ Where the water is clear and cold/ Meet me tonight by the Red River/ and look down into your soul"
-Tom Petty, "Red River," Hypnotic Eye, 2014

[21] "But let's get to the point/ let's roll another joint/ and turn the radio loud,/ I'm too alone to be proud"
-Tom Petty, "You Don't Know How It Feels," Wildflowers, 1994

[22] "You belong among the wildflowers,/ you belong in a boat out at sea./ Sail away, kill off the hours,/ you belong somewhere you feel free"
-Tom Petty, "Wildflowers," Wildflowers, 1994

[23] "And if I never do nothin/ I'm coming back someday/ 'cause you got a heart so big/ it could crush this town/ and I can't hold out forever/ even walls fall down"
-Tom Petty, "Walls (No 3)" She's the One, 1996

[24] "Well I know what's right/ I got just one life/ In a world that

keeps on pushin' me around/ but I'll stand my ground/ and I won't back down."
-Tom Petty, "I Won't Back Down," Full Moon Fever, 1989

[25] "People are what people make 'em,/ and that ain't gonna change./ There ain't nothin' you can do,/nothing you could rearrange/ but I forgive it all/ I forgive it all."
-Tom Petty, "I Forgive it All," 2 (Mudcrutch), 2016

[26] "love isn't easy/ isn't always kind/ but I could have stood there/ lost in your eyes"
-Tom Petty, "Lost in Your Eyes," An American Treasure, 2018 (Outtake, 1974)

[27] "Don't be afraid to live what you believe/ nothin' matters/ (it doesn't matter)/ when you keep a little soul/ nothing really matters anymore"
-Tom Petty, "Keep A Little Soul," An American Treasure, 2018 (Outtake, 1982)

[28] "We were caught up in a barroom fight/ 'til an Indian shot out the lights/ I'm so tired of being tired,/ as sure as night will follow day/ most things I worry about/ never happen anyway"
-Tom Petty, "Crawling Back to You," Wildflowers, 1994

[29] "I threw all I had/ into the sea/ now I want a little back/ this one's for me."
-Tom Petty, "This One's For Me," Echo, 1999

ABOUT THE AUTHOR

Photo by Alethea Phillips

Michelle Lietz (she/her) is an Indigenous American author of mixed Yaqui, European, and Middle Eastern descent originally from the traditional homelands of the Potawatomi in southeast Michigan. She holds a Master of Arts degree in Literature, and her poetry has previously been published in Prairie Fire's "NDN City" issue. *Occasionally Petty* is her first complete poetry publication.